Debbie Duncan's books are
into our anxious culture. She retells Bible stories through the
lens of emotion, in a lively and accessible way. The brilliant,
two-tiered approach means that both little ones and older
children alike will come away with a greater grasp of their
emotional and mental well-being.
Katharine Hill, *UK Director of Care for the Family*

Adults and children will find this series thought-provoking and
encouraging in exploring how we deal with feelings. We often
hide from negative emotions, so books that help children face
them, talk and pray about them, are an invaluable resource to
promote emotional well-being.
Sue Monckton-Rickett, *Chair of the Association of Christian
Counsellors*

Despite the increased focus on mental well-being around us,
we rarely consider the emotional challenges of characters in the
Bible. And yet, their feelings and responses are so helpful for us
as we navigate our own obstacles and opportunities. This series
gives parents and adults the tools to dig deeper with children
and young people, enabling them to relate and learn from the
valuable truths and experiences found in these much loved
stories. These books will build emotional resilience and strong
faith — and are great fun to read. What's not to love?
Cathy Madavan, *Speaker, author, and Kyria Network board
member*

Debbie Duncan's God Cares series brilliantly helps children understand the emotions of Bible characters while encouraging them to explore their own emotions in the face of similar situations. What is more, the books do it in a style that retains the excitement and adventure of the stories themselves. The books also offer practical help to parents and carers as they engage with their children on this voyage of discovery.
Bob Hartman, *Author and performance storyteller*

According to Barnardo's one in ten children have a diagnosable mental health condition and many, while they are undiagnosed, are unhappy and anxious for many reasons in today's world. Early intervention is vital before their feelings become more problematic. Debbie's God Cares series offers a gentle in-road for parents and carers to encourage them to open up about what they are feeling and what is going on in their lives. Learning early on how much God loves them and cares for them can only be a positive. Seeing their own feelings in well-known Bible characters will show them that no matter what the circumstance, God always wins!
Karen Lennie, *Cognitive Behavioural Psychotherapist PG Dip BABCP Member (Accred)*

GOD CARES
WHEN I FEEL DOWN

Jonah and Other Stories

By Debbie Duncan

**CANDLE
BOOKS**

This book is dedicated to Eleanor, safe with Jesus.

Published by
Lion Hudson Limited
Wilkinson House, Jordan Hill Business Park
Banbury Road, Oxford OX2 8DR, England

www.lionhudson.com

ISBN 978 1 78128 377 6

First edition 2020

Acknowledgments
Cover illustration by Anita Belli
With thanks to Joy Wright from Emerge Advocacy for helping and advising on this chapter book.
Scripture quotation on pp. 33–34 taken from The Holy Bible, International Children's Bible® Copyright © 1986, 1988, 1999, 2015 by Tommy Nelson™, a division of Thomas Nelson. Used by permission.
Scripture quotation on p. 45 taken from the Holy Bible, New International Version Anglicised. Copyright © 1979, 1984, 2011 Biblica, formerly International Bible Society. Used by permission of Hodder & Stoughton Ltd, an Hachette UK company. All rights reserved. "NIV" is a registered trademark of Biblica. UK trademark number 1448790.

A catalogue record for this book is available from the British Library

Printed and bound in China, January 2020, LH54

CONTENTS

About the Series

> *"In raising healthy children, it's not enough to just focus on the physical aspect of health. To be truly healthy, a child's emotional health must be nurtured and strengthened. Developing a mental attitude of wellness is also essential. When we adopt an attitude of wellness, we take on a belief that being well is a natural, normal state."*

Jane Sheppard, "A Wellness Approach for Children", *Aspire* **magazine, 9 June 2009**

The *God Cares* series is about providing parents with a biblical approach to discussing emotions and behaviour with their children to provide an attitude of wellness. Children of different ages and at different stages of their emotional development approach things differently, so this series works on two separate levels: **readers aimed at five- to seven-year olds, and chapter books aimed at children aged eight and above**. Please note that children progress at different rates in terms of their reading ability and emotional development, so the age ranges are only a guide for parents and carers.

The Bible stories are retold reflecting on the emotions. Children are encouraged to discuss this and relate the stories to their own situations. Sections at the back provide a reflective space for children, and practical advice for parents and carers.

About the Author

Debbie Duncan, the author of *The Art of Daily Resilience* and *Brave*, is a nurse, a teacher, and the mother of four children. Debbie has considerable insight into what constitutes resilience and bravery: the ability to cope, to stay on course, and to bounce back. In her books she considers what is required for physical, mental, and spiritual durability, interweaving biblical teaching and prayers with personal anecdotes and sound advice. This she now applies specifically to support parents and carers raising children.

Introduction

Even though it was written a very long time ago, the Bible has many stories and parables in it that can help us make sense of the world we live in. That is because it is God's word. The Bible can also help us to understand how we are feeling and how we can cope with those feelings. The story of Jonah and the whale is one of those stories. It is a strange story and you may think it has nothing to do with today or how you are feeling – but it does!

Jonah lived over 2,000 years ago and he even has his own book named after him in the Old Testament of the Bible. Jonah had a difficult time. He ran away from doing what was right, nearly drowned, got swallowed by a whale, and ended up living in a desert. He really didn't want to do what God asked of him, and because he felt guilty, resentful, and confused, he also became sad.

As the story unfolds, each chapter of this book also includes some other Bible stories to help us understand what Jonah was going through, as well as some questions to think about and suggested activities.

We may not be asked to do something like Jonah. However, we might find ourselves in a hard situation, or perhaps someone else is doing something wrong that is affecting us. The difficult feelings that we have aren't always our fault. We can, however, talk to God about them. This is something that Jonah forgot he could do.

After reading the story, discuss it, and how you feel, with your parents or those who care for you. There are some talking points at the end of the book to help you.

CHAPTER ONE

LET'S MEET JONAH

Jonah was God's spokesperson in the northern kingdom of Israel. He believed in God and had promised to serve him. God asked Jonah to travel to the city of Nineveh and tell its people to stop misbehaving and to sort out their lives. You may think there is nothing wrong with that, but to Jonah it was bad news! Jonah knew that if the people changed what they were doing and followed God, then God would forgive them. But Jonah didn't want God to forgive them.

In fact, Jonah just didn't like what God wanted him to do.

Jonah felt that the people of Nineveh should not get a second chance as Nineveh was thought to be a wicked place. It was also the capital of the Assyrian empire, which was one of Israel's fiercest enemies. The Assyrians had been at war with Israel for a long time. After finally defeating Israel, the Assyrians had captured and enslaved its people, and had even brought Israel's other enemies to live in Israel's lands.

You would think that Jonah would trust God and try to forgive the people of Nineveh. After all, God asks us to love everyone, even those who hurt us. But it is a difficult thing to do.

~~~~~~~~~~~~~~~~~~~~~~~~~~~~~~~~~

Jesus told a story about a man who owned a vineyard, and the people who turned against him. A vineyard is a large piece of land where vines grow and produce grapes. When the grapes are ripened by the sun, they are collected and made into wine.

In Jesus' story the owner of the vineyard had to go away. Rather than leave the vines to be destroyed by the wind and rain, he rented it out to some workers. Vines take a long time to grow and need lots of care. It was very important to the man. The workers promised him they would look after the vineyard.

When it was time to collect the grapes, the owner sent his servants to collect them but the workers beat the servants up and refused to give them the fruit. The man sent more servants and the workers even murdered them! So eventually, as he could not go himself, the owner sent his son. The owner thought that the workers would respect his son and pay him what they owed. Instead they killed him too as they wanted to own the vineyard themselves.

Jesus told us this story to help us understand how God feels about his son. God sent many messengers to his people to remind them of his love and forgiveness. The people didn't always listen and finally when God sent his son, Jesus, they killed him. Jesus asked God to forgive them as he died.

You can read the full story in Matthew chapter 21, verses 33–44.

Jonah thought he knew better than God. He also didn't like the Assyrian people so instead of trying to love them he continued to hate them. A bad feeling like hatred can make us sad, as it is not what God wants for us. It is like being bitten by a deadly animal and not getting any help. The poison travels around our body killing good healthy cells and making everything turn bad.

Jonah let his feelings about the Assyrians poison his thinking and he made the wrong decisions. He also broke his promise to God as he wasn't doing what God asked of him. Jonah had a message to share with people he didn't like. He didn't want to pass on this message. He didn't even feel guilty about doing his own thing! Jonah thought he knew best.

Imagine thinking you know better than God. Although Jonah decided to do his own thing, at some point he would be reminded of his promises to God and feel guilty about it.

One of Jesus' friends called Peter also felt guilty. He loved Jesus with all his heart and Jesus was his best friend. If you have a good friend like that, you would never mean to hurt them. You would want everyone to know how special they are.

When Jesus was arrested and taken to jail, his friends became very scared. It's not surprising they were afraid, as the soldiers were fierce-looking with threatening weapons. Peter decided to follow Jesus and see what was happening. He thought that Jesus would save himself and his friends from the Roman soldiers, and he was confused about what was happening. God, however, had an even bigger plan as Jesus was going to save the whole world.

So, watching from afar, Peter lurked in the shadows not wanting to get caught. Eventually he went to stand by a lovely, warm fire because it was a cold night. One of the people standing nearby noticed that Peter didn't look like he was from Jerusalem – she was sure he must know

Jesus. She and others asked Peter three times if he was a friend of Jesus. Each time Peter lied and said, "NO!"

Eventually morning came, and Peter remembered that Jesus had said Peter would pretend he didn't know him. After Jesus was raised from the dead, he saw Peter and told him he forgave him three times, just like Peter lied three times. Jesus knew that Peter would fail. We all fail as we are not perfect. Jesus would have known that Peter needed to hear he was forgiven, or he would carry the terrible feelings of guilt around with him like an extra weight.

Guilt is an awful feeling. If we do not ask for forgiveness, then it is also like the poison from a dangerous animal. It can make us feel useless, sad, and confused.

You can read the full story in Luke chapter 22, verses 54–62.

Jonah, being a stubborn person and thinking he knew better than God, did the opposite of what God told him to do. He travelled to Joppa and organized a lift on a ship to a place called Tarshish, in modern-day Spain. That was no mean feat! There were no sports cars or aeroplanes. Horse and cart, or camel travel would be the best transport across the land. Tarshish was also in the opposite direction to Nineveh. In fact, it was probably 2,500 miles (4,000 km) away from Jonah's home!

God only wanted Jonah to travel 500 miles (800 km) to Nineveh. Jonah chose the furthest place that he could go to because he was trying to run away from God. Jonah soon learned that you can never hide from God. He would have been better off telling God how he really felt. God is the one we should always run to, not the one we run from.

Try drawing something that shows how you feel and tell God about it.

CHAPTER TWO

THE STORM

God loves us and knows everything about us, even the number of hairs on our heads! He also knows if we are trying to hide from him. He wants to be our friend and loves us even more than our parents or the people who care for us do.

Jonah probably thought he was safe. He was in a large ship heading hundreds of miles in the opposite direction from Nineveh, but God knew where Jonah was and what he was up to. Jonah was sleeping at the bottom of the ship when its sailors suddenly found themselves in the middle of an awful storm. These were sailors who really knew what they were doing and were probably not afraid of anything. But they were afraid of the awful storm that God had sent. God had sent the storm to wake Jonah up.

As the sailors threw everything they could overboard to lighten the load of the ship and stop it sinking, Jonah stayed fast asleep. He was hiding from the sailors, God, and even from his own feelings. He must have felt guilty and sad that he wasn't doing what God wanted him to do. Maybe he went to the bottom of the ship to hide from the world around him.

> Maybe you don't go to the bottom of a ship but there is probably a place where you do go to hide or be by yourself. Next time you're there, try asking Jesus to be in there with you. Ask him to show you where he is in your hiding place, and what he wants to say to you.

The sailors kept throwing everything they could find into the sea. They would have thrown the barrels and the ropes, the extra sacks of flour, and the clay jars of food overboard until nothing was left! As they got rid of the extra weight, the sailors prayed and cried out to their own gods to help them. Meanwhile Jonah was still below deck in a deep sleep and hiding from the world. He must have been exhausted coping with his confusing feelings and emotions. He would have also been tired from all the extra travelling he had done. Sometimes when we are very tired, we cannot think straight. Have you ever felt like your thoughts were in a tangle? What advice would you give to Jonah in this situation?

Eventually the ship's captain found Jonah and woke him up. He shouted at Jonah for sleeping while everyone else was running around trying to save the ship and praying for the storm to stop. He told Jonah to pray to God. All around the storm continued to rage as if God was angry with them.

The rest of the crew knew their prayers were not being answered. They wondered if there was someone on the ship who was the reason why they were struggling to save the ship and fighting for their lives. In those days they would cast lots to find that person. It was a little like tossing a coin for heads or tails, or throwing a dice to get a six.

I don't know how the crew did it but they decided the person who was causing the problem was Jonah. They believed God was angry with him.

By this time Jonah was awake, cornered by frightened men asking him lots of questions. Jonah must have been frightened himself. Can you imagine a group of angry, frightened men all shouting at you when you have just woken up from a deep sleep?

The men wanted to know who Jonah was, what country he came from, and why he was travelling. They really wanted to know why Jonah had brought all this trouble upon them. So Jonah told them the whole story; how he came from the land of Israel and how he was trying to hide from the presence of God as he didn't want to go to Nineveh. I expect he wondered if the men would believe him. Perhaps Jonah felt angry that God wanted to rescue his enemy, guilty for not doing what he had promised, tired from all his travelling and thinking, confused, and scared. No wonder he was not happy.

The Bible tells us the story of a man called Elijah. He was like Jonah as he was also God's messenger to people that did not follow God. Elijah lived in the northern part of Israel. The country was ruled by a king and queen who did not believe in God. In fact they built big statues worshipping other gods and told the people of the land to do the same thing. Elijah would not do as they said. He was courageous and warned the people to only follow the true God, even though he knew King Ahab and his wife, Queen Jezebel, would kill him. Elijah was known as "the greatest troublemaker of Israel".

In the end King Ahab and Elijah had a competition to find out who was the true god. The competition – between King Ahab and his men, and Elijah and God – was to see who could cause a huge bonfire to light up and burn without any matches. Elijah strongly believed that God was stronger so when it came to his turn to pray, he poured water over the bonfire to show that God can even set fire to wet wood. God sent fire and burnt the wood. It was better than the greatest firework display.

Queen Jezebel was so angry that she killed all of King Ahab's men and tried to kill Elijah too. Elijah ran away to the countryside and hid. He was so sad that he wanted to die. He probably thought that after the competition he would be safe. Elijah sat down under a broom tree and told God he wanted to die. God didn't tell him not to be silly or to have more faith. God knew that Elijah was shattered and needed to rest. He looked after him, providing him with food and water. Eventually Elijah spoke to God and told him how confused and afraid he was. God reminded Elijah that he was not alone and that he could trust God and tell him how he felt. God cares.

You can read the full story in 1 Kings chapters 18 and 19.

The sailors kept asking Jonah questions. They even asked Jonah, "What shall we do to you, that the storm may cease?"

Jonah must have guessed what was coming, but instead of stopping and asking God to forgive him, he kept running. He told the sailors to take him up to the deck and throw him into the sea. He believed that, if they did that, the storm would stop and the sea would return to normal. He knew the storm was his fault. The sailors were kind men and didn't want to throw Jonah overboard. They even tried to row the ship to the shore, but they couldn't manage it. The storm was too strong.

The sailors all called out to God to save them and not let them die because of Jonah. You would think that Jonah would have prayed to God for help. Instead the sailors prayed. Jonah was disobedient to God. He did not do what God asked of him. The sailors, who did not really know God, did what he told them to. The sailors prayed with all their hearts while Jonah did not.

The sailors had tried everything. They could do nothing else to save the boat or themselves, so they threw Jonah into the sea.

The sailors were worried about Jonah and had tried to do what was right for him, but Jonah didn't seem to care for them. Sometimes when we are angry, guilty, or sad, we do not do what is right as our feelings can make us confused. Jonah should have spoken to God about how he was feeling. When we feel sad or confused, we can do the same, even if we don't know God that well.

Have you ever thought that things were so complicated that you felt overwhelmed and hopeless?
What happened? How did you get through it? Having these feelings doesn't mean we have no faith or that we should be ashamed. As we continue Jonah's story, we'll see how God works in and through all these feelings and situations in the lives of the people in the Bible. He does the same in our lives today too.
Try writing down how you are feeling and then share what you have written with someone you trust.

CHAPTER THREE

INSIDE THE WHALE

As soon as Jonah was thrown into the sea, the terrible storm instantly stopped. The huge waves became still and all the men in the boat knew they were saved. These brave, strong sailors, who believed in other gods, suddenly became afraid of our God. They knew that even the waves and winds obeyed God. The men offered a sacrifice to God, which in those days was a way of showing you were really serious about what you were saying. They made promises to serve God for the rest of their lives.

In the New Testament part of the Bible, Jesus showed us that he is also God when he calmed the raging storm. He had been teaching the people around him about God all day. People wanted to hear Jesus as he reminded them that God was interested in them. He explained things that even the priests, who were meant to know about God, didn't know. It was tiring, though, spending all day surrounded by people. When the evening came, Jesus asked his friends if they could leave all the people on the shore and get into a boat so he could have some space. Some of his friends had their own boats because they were fishermen, so that's what they did. Soon Jesus was resting on some cushions and sound asleep.

Jesus was sleeping in the boat in the middle of a massive lake called the Sea of Galilee. People called it a sea because it is huge. You can still visit it today. Because it is in the middle of a deep valley, cold air sometimes comes down from the hilltops and hits the warm winds across the sea. This causes storms to suddenly appear. One minute you can be out on the peaceful water, enjoying the quiet, and then suddenly the sky goes dark and waves up to 10 feet (3 metres) tall start hammering your boat. That's what happened to Jesus and his friends. All they could see was the waves. All they could hear was the storm. Some of the disciples were experienced fishermen but they were afraid of this storm. They did what many of us do when things suddenly go wrong – they turned to Jesus for help.

The disciples woke up Jesus as they were afraid. Jesus got up and commanded the wind to be still. The storm ended. Everything became calm and the disciples were amazed. They were reminded that Jesus could calm the wind and waves.

You can read the full story in Matthew chapter 8, verses 23–27.

Although God wanted Jonah to go to Nineveh to show the people there that they could be forgiven and serve him, he was also able to save the sailors on the boat. God can bring good out of something that could have been bad. He is, after all, God, who can control the winds and the rain. Even if we don't obey God, or are not sure where he is in our situation, God will still be at work all around us. It wasn't part of God's plan that Jonah would end up on the boat but he still used it for good. If you feel that you have gone off course in life, do not worry. God always has a way to reach you and others around you.

Jonah, in the meantime, was trying to stay alive in the middle of the sea. He knew that this had happened because he was running away from God. But God wasn't punishing Jonah, even though it might have felt like it. He was giving Jonah a way back to him. God loved Jonah so much and was not willing to give up on him, so he sent an enormous beast of a sea creature to rescue him. (We will call it a whale, but we are not sure what it was.) Jonah didn't jump on its back and ride it through the waves, or even swim beside it like a dolphin. Jonah was swallowed alive by the whale!

It must have been a huge whale to be able to swallow Jonah whole. It must have had a large mouth and a huge stomach. Can you imagine how scary being swallowed by a whale would be? First you would fear all the rows of little teeth. I wonder if Jonah had scratches on his arms and legs? I'm sure there would have been other things swallowed at the same time. Jonah must have been really scared that he would drown. He would not have been able to see anything but he would have smelt the whale's foul stomach and felt the freezing cold water swirling around him. It would not have been fun being swallowed, scraped and scratched, and squashed into the whale's stomach.

For three whole days and nights Jonah was stuck in a cold, smelly, dark, scary pit. He was all alone. It's such a difficult place to imagine. Perhaps it reflected a little of how Jonah felt. Sadness and depression are like a deep pit where you feel you cannot get out, like being trapped in a strange place we don't understand. You may wonder if you can live in a whale's stomach – scientists say that a person could live in the stomach of a whale as long as there was air and they were not attacked by digestive juices. It was a strange situation but

God was trying to get Jonah's attention. Jonah must have known that God was in control because he would have heard all the stories about God as he was growing up! Jonah was probably scared. It would have been a terrible place to be.

~~~~~~~~~~~~~~~~~~~~~~~~~~~~~~~~~~~~~~~

When Jesus died on the cross, like Jonah he spent three days and nights in the worst place imaginable – until he came alive again. Jesus died because he wanted us to be able to be friends with God. He took our punishment so that God can forgive us. Unlike Jonah, Jesus was not running away from God or feeling sorry for himself. He chose to die for us so we can live with God forever.

We all do things that are wrong. We all do things that our parents or teachers ask us not to do. That is because God made a perfect world but humans decided they knew better. The first humans were called Adam and Eve and although at first they lived in a perfect relationship with God, they spoilt this by going their own way and not trusting in what he told them would be best for them. They were tempted to go against God and they gave in to that temptation.

This broken relationship affected the whole of creation and opened the way for evil to be at work in the world. But the good thing is that God loves us, his creation, so much that he didn't leave us alone in this mess. God the Father, Son, and Holy Spirit had a plan to bring us back into that close relationship with God that he always meant for us to have. God knew the only way he could be our friend again was if someone was punished for what happened. Jesus agreed to take the punishment. His death means we can be forgiven for all the badness in the world. All we have to do is accept the gift of what Jesus has done for us.

~~~~~~

After all those miles travelling, being in the worst storm imaginable, and then being trapped for three days in a really smelly whale, Jonah prayed to God and finally asked for help. He was probably hungry, tired, battered, and unhappy. When he prayed to God he even said he was covered in seaweed! This is Jonah's prayer from the bottom of the sea:

"I was in danger.
So, I called to the Lord,
and he answered me.
I was about to die.
So I cried to you,
and you heard my voice.
You threw me into the sea.
I went down, down into the deep sea.
The water was all around me.
Your powerful waves flowed over me.
I said, 'I was driven out of your presence.
But I hope to see your Holy Temple again.'
The waters of the sea closed over me.
I was about to die.
The deep sea was all around me.
Seaweed wrapped around my head.
I went down to where the mountains of
the sea start to rise.

I thought I was locked in this prison forever.
But you saved me from death,
> *Lord my God.*

When my life had almost gone,
> *I remembered the Lord.*
Lord, I prayed to you.
> *And you heard my prayers in your*
> *Holy Temple.*

People who worship useless idols
> *give up their loyalty to you.*
Lord, I will praise and thank you
> *while I give sacrifices to you.*
I will make promises to you.
> *And I will do what I promise.*
Salvation comes from the Lord!"

Jonah 2:2–9

We might feel like this, but God will never drive us from his presence. God shares our pain in suffering, he cries with us, is close to us, and journeys through it with us.

Jonah had been really determined that he was doing his own thing and didn't need God's help!

After being thrown overboard and then being swallowed by a huge whale, he finally asked God to help him escape. God heard his prayer and made the whale release him on the seashore. God hears all our prayers. Sometimes he does not answer them in the way we want. That is because he loves us and knows what is best for us.

Jonah promised God he would do what God had asked of him. God still had a plan for this man called Jonah — and Jonah ended up being washed up on the seashore near Nineveh.

Why don't you sit for a minute and thank God for what he has done for you? Think of all the times he has helped you when things have gone wrong.

CHAPTER FOUR

THE CITY OF NINEVEH

Jonah was called Jonah for a reason. It wasn't because his parents just liked the name, although it is a great name. In the Bible, people's names are important because they mean something. Jonah's name means "dove".

~~~~~~~~~~~~~~~~~~~~~~

In the story of Noah's Ark, which is found in the first book of the Bible, there is an important dove. The people during

Noah's time disobeyed God, so he sent a flood to destroy the land. Only two of every animal, and Noah and his family survived. This was because God told Noah to build a large boat called an ark, which saved them all from drowning.

After the rains stopped, the ark landed on a mountain. Noah sent out a raven first and then a dove to see how far the floodwaters had gone down. The first time the dove found nothing and returned to the ark. The second time the dove brought back an olive leaf, as a sign of God's peace, and Noah knew that life had begun again on Earth.

You can read the full story in Genesis chapter 6 verse 9 – chapter 8.

~~~~~~~~~~~~~~~~~~~~~~~~~~~~~~~~~~~~~

Jonah was to be like a dove, bringing God's message of peace and hope to the people of Nineveh if they followed him. So God made the whale release Jonah and told him again to travel to Nineveh. He must warn the people there of the trouble they were in so they could ask for God's help. This time Jonah did what God wanted him to do. He travelled to Nineveh, which was still quite a distance away. In fact, it took a whole day to get there. Nineveh was also a very large city. It was so large, it would have taken three days just to walk through it. Jonah went into the city shouting God's warning that in forty days Nineveh would be destroyed.

The people pleaded to God for help. God wanted to know they were serious about what they were saying so Jonah told them they should wear sackcloths – clothes made from material that is hairy, itchy, and smelly. They all wore the worst clothes they had to show God they were sad. They were pleading for God's help and wanted him to know they were serious about what they were praying for. Even the king took off his posh robes and wore a sackcloth, covering his face in black ashes from a fire. The king issued an order that the people in the city must "fast", meaning they could have nothing to eat or drink for a period of time. Even the animals, including the sheep and cows, were not allowed to eat or drink. The people also covered the animals in sackcloths.

In those days fasting was an outward sign that people were serious about wanting God to forgive them and asking for God's help. We do not need to do that. We can simply talk to God and he sees how serious we are.

Can you imagine a whole city, adults and children, dressing up in the worst clothes imaginable and all crying out to God? That's what happened. The city turned to God and asked for forgiveness, and God heard them. The city would not need to be destroyed. God hears every person who calls out to him, and, true to his promise, he forgives him or her.

If you knew so many people had turned to God, maybe you would celebrate – even have a party! But not Jonah. He still thought he knew better than God and became angry. He was so upset that he wanted to die. Despite knowing about God, being rescued from an awful storm, sinking into an ocean, being covered in seaweed, seeing the inside of a whale, and seeing a whole city turn to God, Jonah was unhappy. He thought the people of Nineveh didn't deserve to be forgiven by God. He still thought he knew best.

Jonah left Nineveh and built himself somewhere to stay east of the city. He decided to watch what he hoped would be the destruction of Nineveh. The shelter couldn't have been a good one; I doubt Jonah could build houses like ours. Where would he get all the bricks, cement, or roof tiles? He would have used what was lying around.

As it was not a good shelter and did not protect Jonah from the hot sun, the God of all the earth, sky, and sea made a leafy plant to grow over Jonah's shelter to give him some shade. Meanwhile, Jonah waited to see Nineveh burn. But God saved the city and waited to see if Jonah would understand how badly he had behaved.

The city of Nineveh was the capital city of the Assyrian empire. It was an important place and people wanted to live there. Historians think that the Assyrian people were the first to invent door locks, as well as some of the first clocks, libraries, roads, and even flushing toilets! Even today, after hundreds of years, you can still see the ruins of the city. The Bible tells us that there were more than 120,000 people in Nineveh and all their animals (Jonah 4:11). The problem was that Jonah cared more for his plant than the men, women, and children who needed God. If he really cared for the people, he would have told them straight away that God forgave them.

So, early the next morning, as the sun was rising, God sent a worm or a maggot to chomp on the plant's root. The plant needed deep roots to survive in the hot sun, so after the worm ate its root, the plant withered and died. Then, when the sun had risen, God also provided a scorching east wind. The sun blazed on Jonah's head so that he grew faint. Jonah was so sad he wanted to die. He felt so miserable that if you had met him you would have thought that his favourite pet or even his granny or grandad had died. He mourned the plant that he had only known for a day.

God wanted to get Jonah's attention. God often wants us to see his heart and his plans – to be more like him, more like he created us to be. God wanted Jonah to realize he had sinned so he could turn away from it, not because he wanted Jonah to feel bad about himself. Jonah was full of envy, jealousy, and anger. Instead of talking to God about how he was feeling, Jonah became sadder and more depressed. You would think he would move away from the harmful sun, build a proper shelter, or even go into the city to find somewhere to stay. Instead he stayed where he was in the hot sun getting more and more sunburnt. In fact, he felt so sad that he asked God to let him die. Sometimes we are so confused and sad that we don't know what the best thing is to do. Our feelings make it hard for us to make decisions.

So God challenged Jonah. He asked, "Is it right for you to be angry about the plant?"

Jonah replied, "It is and I'm so angry I wish I were dead."

Again God challenged Jonah. He said, "You have been so worried about this plant, even though you did not look after it or make it grow. It sprang up overnight and died overnight. Am I not allowed to care for the great city of Nineveh, in which there are more than 120,000 people who cannot tell their right hand from their left?"

God reminded Jonah that it was wrong to be concerned by a plant he had not even planted or helped grow. God used the plant as a symbol to help Jonah understand. Jonah cared for the plant, even though he had not grown it, because it gave him shade. God cared for the people of Nineveh, who he created, even though they disobeyed him.

We do not know what happened next. Perhaps Jonah headed into Nineveh to meet the people who now believed in God. Perhaps he went home challenged by God for his wrong attitude. What we do know is that God, who gave the people of Nineveh a second chance, was also interested in seeing Jonah change. God wanted to help Jonah for he loved him and only wanted the best for him.

The story ends with Jonah talking to God about what had happened and that is a good place to end any story.

Talking to God about things is always good but it can be hard to know where to start. If you are unsure about how to pray, then thank God for one thing you are grateful for. You can then tell him you are sorry for the wrong things you have done, and ask for his help.

CHAPTER FIVE

WHAT YOU CAN DO

The story of Jonah is a helpful story as we are reminded that we can all feel sad or have a low mood. This is normal. There are also many things that can make us feel sad.

Think of the story. What made Jonah sad? Jonah was sad because God wanted him to do something he didn't agree with. Jonah didn't like the idea that God was giving the people of Nineveh a second chance. Jonah didn't want to do that and tried to run away from God. We need to remember that God knows what is best for us — after all, he is God! If we don't live as he wants us to, then we can become sad. We can also be sad because of difficult circumstances or because other people do things that affect us.

Jonah also lost something he loved. He really loved his plant. That is a little strange, but he talked to the plant and spent a day watching it grow. It gave him shelter and made him feel safe. The Bible says:

> *"Then the Lord God provided a leafy plant and made it grow up over Jonah to give shade for his head to ease his discomfort, and Jonah was very happy about the plant."*

Jonah 4: 6–8

We often love things that make us happy, especially if they bring us comfort or provide distraction during difficult times. It can be something like a special soft toy, a certain place where we feel safe, being around people who make us feel good, or maybe even a particular song. These things are important when times are tough.

When the plant died, Jonah's sadness got worse. Jonah became depressed. Depression is different from just feeling sad or low as it lasts for a much longer time. Just because someone feels sad, lonely, or they are grumpy does not mean he or she has depression.

Although we know why Jonah felt low and was depressed, we often do not know the reason why people develop depression. These feelings can be caused by any combination of factors, such as physical illness or moving to a new house or school.

Our parents or teachers may be able to tell we have depression by a range of behaviours we can show. You may need someone to explain these to you. Doctors and nurses call these signs and symptoms. Some of the signs and symptoms are difficult to spot. We don't always know what exactly someone is feeling.

The signs and symptoms of depression include:

- No interest in eating or drinking, or eating too much
- Not being able to sleep, or sleeping all the time

What You Can Do

- Feelings of sadness or hopelessness that don't go away
- Finding it hard to concentrate
- Feeling tired all the time
- Becoming angry or sad for no reason
- Having a sore stomach or headaches
- Not wanting to see our friends or play.

If we feel like this then we need to tell someone we trust. Your parents or guardians will probably take you to see a doctor to help find out what is wrong. Together you will be able to find out how to treat how you are feeling.

Talking Points

The following questions are here to help you think about things. They are ideas for you to chat about with your parents, a teacher, someone at church, or another adult you trust.

Questions:

- Why did Jonah not want to do what God asked of him?
- What made Jonah so sad?
- What can you do if you feel sad?
- What do you think of the way Jonah handled his feelings? What did he do well and what could he have done differently?
- How do you normally handle difficult feelings?
- What do you do when you have the types of feelings Jonah had?

Maybe there is a specific reason why you are sad, angry, or resentful. It is best to talk about it to an adult you can trust. There are also a few other things you can do. The following list suggests a few things you can do when you are feeling sad:

WHAT YOU CAN DO

- Talk to people you trust.
- Talk to God.
- Keep a journal and write things down. Share it with your parents.
- Write a list of all the things that you are thankful for.
- Make sure you are sleeping properly.
- Make sure you are eating and drinking properly.

Here is a prayer you can pray. You may want to say your own prayer like Jonah did or write one down.

Prayer

Dear God,

Thank you that you are interested in me.
You love me and want the best for me.
You made me and know everything about me.

Help me to trust you and talk to you, no matter how I feel. I know that even Jesus felt sad and understands how I feel.

Thank you that you are with me wherever I am. Help me to remember that even if I feel sad, you are with me. That is a fact.

Help me to remember Jesus and that he died for me.

Amen

What You Can Do

Remember:

- God cares for you even when you are feeling down.
- Anyone can feel sad or depressed.
- There are lots of things you can do to help yourself feel better.
- You don't need to feel that you have to face things alone.
- You can always talk to God, family, and friends.

CHAPTER SIX

PRACTICAL HELP

for Parents, Carers, and Teachers

It is important to teach children that it is normal to have episodes when we feel sad or low. We all experience sadness in response to life's usual events such as saying goodbye to friends as we move to a new house.

Children as young as five years old can develop depression if it is not identified as early as possible. Depression is a long-lasting, persistent sadness where individuals may also experience suicidal feelings. We do not always know the cause.

Sometimes depression develops because of the cumulative effect of childhood experiences and events that all add up to make things feel worse. Whatever the cause, depression can make some feel a deep emotional pain. It should be considered as important as the pain you have after breaking an arm or during a serious illness. Children are also more prone to depression as many are growing up in poverty and experiencing vulnerability.

The symptoms of childhood depression are similar to those of adults, but children may have difficulty identifying and describing how they really feel.

The signs and symptoms of depression include:

- Sustained changes in appetite – either increased or decreased appetite
- Sustained changes in sleep patterns
- Continuous feelings of sadness or hopelessness
- Difficulty concentrating
- Fatigue and tiredness
- Feelings of worthlessness or guilt
- Difficulty with concentration
- Acute mood swings
- Irritability or anger

- Physical complaints; these can range from stomach aches to headaches
- Reduced interest in friends and family
- Withdrawal from interacting with others
- Thoughts of death or suicide
- Vocal outbursts or crying.

If a child's symptoms last for at least two weeks, then he or she needs to see a doctor. The doctor will want to ensure there are no physical reasons for the symptoms. The child will also need a mental health evaluation much like a physical check-up. Once the medical team have this information, they can use it to determine what is wrong, and can work with the family to provide treatment.

In some cases we just cannot prevent our children from developing depression, but there are some basic things we can do to support good mental health. These include a healthy diet, enough sleep, exercise, and positive relationships with other children and supportive adults.

Here are some suggestions:

- Help to establish stability early in life. That may mean avoid moving homes and schools too often. Sometimes we cannot stop this happening, so plan well and ensure a child is involved in any decisions about future moves.

- Encourage strong relationships with additional caring adults, such as relatives, teachers, and members of your church.
  This means a child will always have people they can talk to.

- Encourage a child to be open and honest about what is going on in their lives.
  This includes with their parents, siblings, and God. Researchers suggest that we should encourage children to be open and honest about how they feel.

- Let a child experience life. We live in a broken world and sad things happen.
  We cannot always shelter people from the experiences of life. Although it is painful to see a child suffer a little disappointment now, it will help them deal with more intense frustration and disappointment in the future.

- Let a child know that Jesus understands how they feel. Jesus was upset and cried when he knew his friend had died. If Jesus did that, so can we.

- Children are naturally resilient. Help foster this by ensuring they have support for their physical, mental, and spiritual health. Encourage a healthy lifestyle, incorporating good nutrition, sleep, and exercise. Support them in coping with stress and help them grow in their faith.
- Seek help when you are concerned. Sometimes you may not be able to exactly express why you are concerned but God gives us intuition.
- If you can, reduce a child's exposure to external pressures and stressors. This may include supporting them to identify these stressors and to learn how to cope with them.
- Limit screen time and encourage physical activity.
- Support a child in developing a sense of identity and emotional intelligence.
- Share your own ups and downs with a child in an age-appropriate way. It's good for a child to see how their parents navigate the storms of life, giving them a model to follow. Even if we don't handle things well, we can talk to children about this and talk over what we could do differently next time.

- Try to keep a balance so that a child knows they are more than their issues and will still get adult attention even when they are not struggling.

There are therefore many things we can do to prevent depression or to support people coping with it. Treatment is dependent on the cause of depression. This may include treating any medical condition that causes or worsens depression. An example is the disorder hypothyroidism where people lack the hormone thyroxine. Other treatments are what we call "supportive therapy", such as lifestyle and behavioural changes, psychotherapy, complementary treatments, and medication for moderate to severe depression. If symptoms are severe then sometimes the child must go into hospital for additional medical care.

We may feel that we must also cope with the stigma associated with mental illness. Thankfully this is becoming less of a problem as society seeks to understand that mental illness is as common as physical illness. It is important that you don't feel guilty or believe that your child's illness is your fault. There are lots of available resources as you make this journey. If your child is struggling, you will need support as you help them through this time. Alongside this, be aware of your child's need for confidentiality and think carefully about who to share the situation with. Not everyone in the family may need to know all the details about what's going on, for example. Choose one or two people that you feel you can talk to, and check with your child that they are happy for you to confide in those people about the situation.

Resources

Action for Children:
https://www.actionforchildren.org.uk/support-for-parents/children-s-mental-health/how-can-you-help-with-children-and-young-peoples-mental-health/mental-health-resources-and-information/

Association of Christian Counsellors:
https://www.acc-uk.org/find-a-counsellor/search-for-a-counsellor.html

Care for the Family – parent support:
https://www.careforthefamily.org.uk/family-life/parent-support

Childline:
https://www.childline.org.uk/info-advice/your-feelings/feelings-emotions/depression-feeling-sad

Other Titles in the Series

Readers:
God Cares When I am Afraid: Jesus Calms the Storm
God Cares When I am Strong: Friends in the Fire

Chapter Books:
God Cares When I am Anxious: Moses and Other Stories

Acknowledgments

I want to thank my husband Malcolm, Matthew and Eve, Benjamin and Ellie, Anna and Jacob, Riodhna, Rob and Emily – our family – for all their love and care while writing this series.

I also want to thank Anita Belli who is so gifted at illustration and captured what I was trying to say in the readers.

I also want to thank the Lion Hudson family: Suzanne Wilson-Higgins for that initial conversation, commissioning editor Deborah Lock for her patience, Jacqui Crawford for the design and layout, and Stella Caldwell and Eva Rojas for advice and poetry help on the readers (some of the lines are Eva's). You are just a few of the family!

Thank you.